THE CICADA

ROSS E. HUTCHINS
ILLUSTRATED BY ARVIS L. STEWART

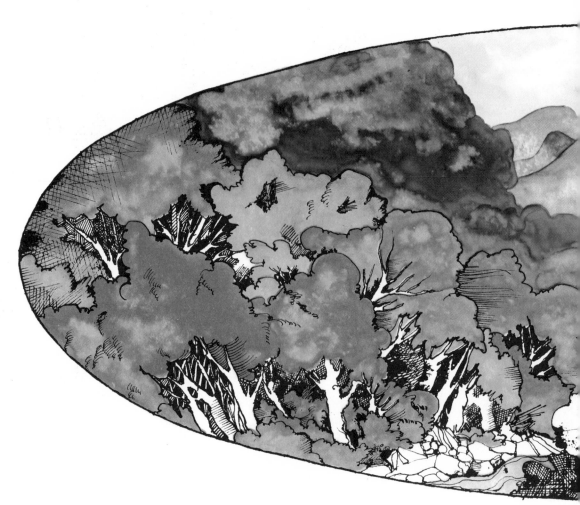

▲ ADDISON-WESLEY

the Cicada

An Addisonian Press Book

Addison-Wesley Publishing Company, Inc.
Reading, Massachusetts 01867
Library of Congress Catalog Card Number 9940
Printed in the United States of America
SBN: 201-03102-7

Hidden below the steep slopes of Clingman's Dome which rises 6,642 feet above sea level in the Great Smoky Mountains, there is a secluded valley. It is known as Little River Valley and no one lives there now. In spring, rhododendrons and dogwoods bloom along the streams while yellow lady's-slippers and white trilliums thrive in the shade of the deeper forest. In some places beautiful waterfalls tumble down the mountainsides.

When autumn arrives in Little Valley with its frosty nights, the maples and oaks turn golden and scarlet, dropping their leaves at last upon the ground or into the streams where they float along like bits of brightly colored paper. It is now late May in the mountains. Summer has at last arrived and the weather is warm. Tiger swallowtail butterflies flutter through the forest and across the river. Chipmunks, as usual, are busily searching for nuts and seeds on the forest floor. Everywhere there are signs of life.

During the past night the forest was silent except for the calls of owls and the sounds of the tumbling river. Now the sun is high above the mountains and its rays reach down into the valley, flooding it with warmth.

Suddenly, a shrill, drumming noise echoes through the forest. It is the call of the first cicada (suh KAY duh). Within a few minutes thousands of other cicadas begin to sing and, shortly, the forest rings with sound.

The sun's heat has warmed the cicadas' bodies and now they perch in the trees and sing. The forest along Little River vibrates with their songs. The din drowns out all other sounds of the forest so that no longer can one hear the roaring of the river nor the songs of birds in the trees.

This is the year of the cicadas, the time when they all come up out of their underground cells to sing in the summer sun.

For 17 years the cicadas have dwelled in the earth, but this is the summer when they will all crawl up out of their tunnels and develop wings. For a few weeks the males will sing in the trees, but the females will remain silent. During that time they will mate and the females will lay their eggs in the twigs of the trees. Thus making sure that when another 17 years have passed there will be another generation of cicadas to fill the forest of Little River Valley with song.

Each cicada is an inch and a half long and its eyes are bright red. It has four cellophane-like wings which it folds roof-like over its back. These wings have orange-red borders and, near the tip of one, there is a dark W. On the underside of the cicada's body, if it is a male, there is a pair of drum-like singing organs. When singing, these organs vibrate in and out very rapidly, making a loud crackling or buzzing sound. The drumming sound can be heard for a great distance.

Today, along Little River, the trees are filled with cicadas. They perch by the thousands in every tree and bush, the males all sounding their drums.

But their songs have attracted enemies. Jays, always hungry, arrive and capture many of them. The birds dart down and grasp them in their sharp beaks, carrying them off to be eaten in the nearby trees. Other birds, too, are attracted, and they also take their toll. Yet, it is Nature's way that although many will be destroyed by enemies, more than enough will survive to reproduce their kind.

Growing along Little River there is a large sycamore tree, its great trunk rising gracefully beside the stream. In this tree are many singing cicadas.

On one leaf, about ten feet above the ground, perches a male cicada. Its drumming organs give off a loud, rasping call. Suddenly, from across the stream, there darts a large wasp. It has been attracted by the sound.

The wasp, nearly two inches long, is a female cicada-killer. It is one of the largest of all wasps. She darts down and grasps the male cicada singing on the sycamore leaf. One moment the cicada is singing on the leaf; the next moment there is a loud screech and then it is silent.

Both wasp and cicada tumble to the ground.

The unfortunate cicada flutters its powerful wings but the great wasp is very strong and quickly stabs it with its needle-like sting, injecting a powerful poison.

The wasp's sting rapidly paralyzes the unfortunate cicada and it stops struggling. It is not dead but is unable to move its wings or legs. The cicada-killer wasp has captured its prize but she now has a problem. She has already dug her nest tunnel in the ground a hundred feet away across the stream to which she must carry her prize. The cicada is larger and heavier than the wasp and the wasp cannot lift it off of the ground no matter how hard she beats her wings.

Satisfied that the captured cicada is completely
inactive the wasp grasps it in her jaws and
begins dragging it along the ground toward a
small bush. When she reaches the bush she
hauls the inactive cicada up the stem. It is
hard work but she is very strong.

About two feet above the ground the wasp
stops and rests for awhile. Then she straddles
her prey and flies away with it. The wasp
could not have air-lifted the heavy cicada
directly off of the ground but, once in the air,
she apparently carries it with ease.

Still carrying the paralyzed cicada suspended beneath her body, the wasp flies across the stream and into the woods. There, beneath a dog-hobble bush, she circles a patch of sandy ground. Satisfied that this is her nest area she quickly finds the tunnel she has already dug in the soft ground and alights nearby. The opening into the tunnel is half an inch in diameter and in front of it is a pile of fresh earth.

Dropping the paralyzed cicada near the tunnel entrance, the wasp runs rapidly about and examines the area. She wants to make sure that nothing has bothered her nest while she has been away hunting. Certain, at last, that all is well she returns to her prize and drags it into the tunnel.

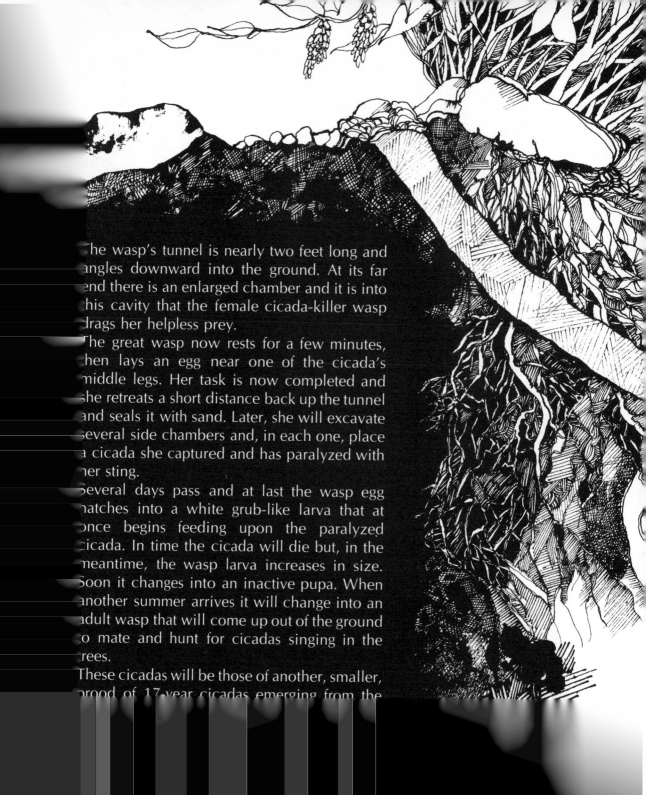

The wasp's tunnel is nearly two feet long and angles downward into the ground. At its far end there is an enlarged chamber and it is into this cavity that the female cicada-killer wasp drags her helpless prey.

The great wasp now rests for a few minutes, then lays an egg near one of the cicada's middle legs. Her task is now completed and she retreats a short distance back up the tunnel and seals it with sand. Later, she will excavate several side chambers and, in each one, place a cicada she captured and has paralyzed with her sting.

Several days pass and at last the wasp egg hatches into a white grub-like larva that at once begins feeding upon the paralyzed cicada. In time the cicada will die but, in the meantime, the wasp larva increases in size. Soon it changes into an inactive pupa. When another summer arrives it will change into an adult wasp that will come up out of the ground to mate and hunt for cicadas singing in the trees.

These cicadas will be those of another, smaller, brood of 17-year cicadas emerging from the

Today as I walk through the forest of Little River Valley I marvel at the sound of the singing cicadas. The air seems filled with noise coming from every direction.

Here on a twig is a male cicada in the act of singing, and I can see its body vibrate or tremble each time it gives forth its rasping call. Curious, I pluck the cicada up in my fingers in order to examine it more closely. It flutters its transparent wings and makes a screeching sound.

Turning the strange insect up-side-down I see that it has a pair of shell-like drumming organs near the base of its body. These, I know, are the source of its loud song. Attached to the inner surface of each drum there is a powerful muscle. When these muscles jerk very rapidly the drums snap in and out, making loud buzzing sounds. That is the song of the male cicada. He sings to attract his mate.

The cicadas singing in the trees along Little River seem to have no cares, but the truth is that they have only a few weeks to find mates and lay their eggs. During this time they will eat very little. Sometimes they pierce tender twigs with their tube-like mouthparts and suck out the sap, but this does not occur very often. They have no true jaws and so cannot chew and eat leaves as do many other kinds of insects.

As the days pass the males continue to sing. Eventually they find mates and, shortly, the females begin laying their eggs in the twigs of the trees.

Anxious to see, at first hand, a female in the act of laying her eggs, I watch the cicadas. Examining many of the insects I, at last, find a female that I suspect is preparing to insert her eggs in the twig of a small tree beside the river. Fortunately, I can watch the cicada while seated comfortably on a large boulder.

I lean forward to observe the insect more closely but she is not alarmed. She is concerned only with the laying of her eggs.

With my eyes only a few inches away I watch in fascination as the cicada pushes her sharp spear-like egg-laying tube into the twig. Then she pauses for awhile but I know that eggs are being pushed out of the tip of her egg-tube and into a pocket in the wood.

20

After remaining motionless for a few minutes the cicada withdraws her egg-tube from the twig and crawls forward for about an inch. Then she thrusts the tube into the wood again. Once more she is quiet as her eggs are laid. This process is repeated several times but at last the cicada is alarmed by my presence and flies away through the forest. She will probably lay more eggs, perhaps as many as five hundred, in the twigs of other trees.

21

After the female cicada has gone, I split open
the twig with my pocket knife, finding several
tiny pockets in the wood, each filled with
slender, white eggs. They are lined up in rows,
side by side, and when I look at them through
my hand lens I see that each pocket contains
about twenty-five eggs, each one about one-
twelfth of an inch long.

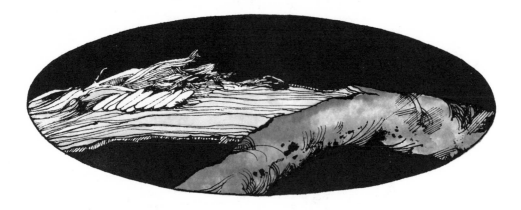

And so I walk down the river, knowing that I
have seen how a new generation of cicadas
begins, a generation that will sing in the summer sun 17 long years from now.
About six weeks have passed and the valley of
Little River no longer echoes with the songs of
cicadas. They are all dead, many of them captured by birds and wasps. Their work was
finished when they all had mated and laid
their eggs. Pierced by the egg-tubes of the
female cicadas, many of the twigs are now
dead, their leaves withered. Yet in almost
every one there are hidden clusters of cicada
eggs, safe from enemies.

Soon, warmed by the summer sun, the eggs
will begin to hatch.
The time is now mid-July.
On the mountainsides the sourwoods are
blooming, their attractive little flowers strung
in rows along the twigs. Acorns are forming on
the oaks and the seed balls of the sycamores
hang suspended from the trees' higher
branches.

Hidden within the twigs of various trees the cicada eggs are hatching. One by one the young nymphs break out of their shells by twisting motions of their bodies. They are white and ant-like in form. Once out of their shells the nymphs crawl rapidly about on the twigs. After awhile they drop off, falling through the air as lightly as thistle down.

The young cicada nymphs are strange-looking little insects. They are blind and only one-sixteenth of an inch long. Their front legs are spiny, well fitted for digging in the earth.

After alighting upon the ground they crawl rapidly about for awhile. When they find cracks in the ground they quickly dig in and disappear. They must dig in within a few minutes, otherwise the hot sun will kill them. A number of the cicada nymphs have burrowed into the ground beneath a small oak. In the dark world below the earth's surface they dig only downward. Using their spiny front legs like picks and shovels they dig slowly through the soil. Sometimes their paths are blocked by small roots or stones, but they go around them, always digging deeper into the ground.

A few of the nymphs make the mistake of burrowing into underground ant nests where they are quickly captured and eaten. A few others are eaten by beetle larvae.

Even in the dark underground world there are many enemies.

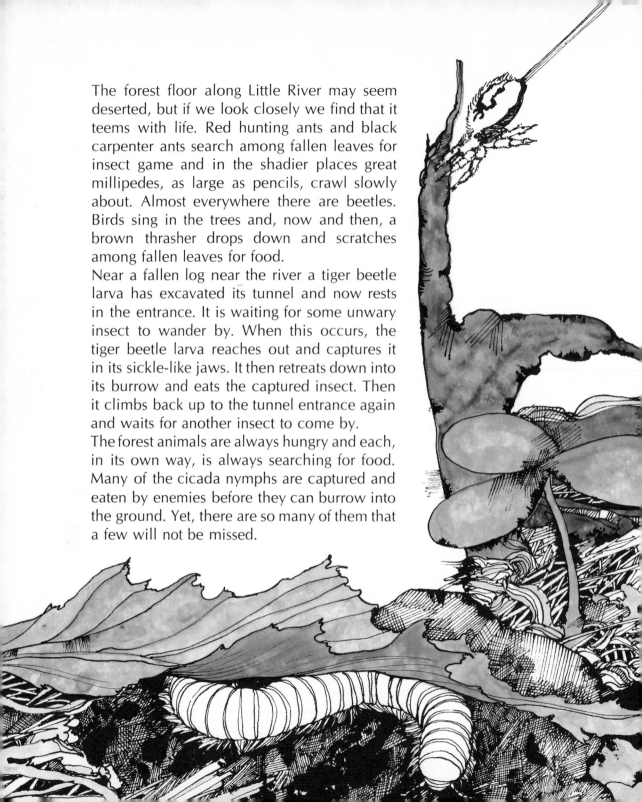

The forest floor along Little River may seem deserted, but if we look closely we find that it teems with life. Red hunting ants and black carpenter ants search among fallen leaves for insect game and in the shadier places great millipedes, as large as pencils, crawl slowly about. Almost everywhere there are beetles. Birds sing in the trees and, now and then, a brown thrasher drops down and scratches among fallen leaves for food.

Near a fallen log near the river a tiger beetle larva has excavated its tunnel and now rests in the entrance. It is waiting for some unwary insect to wander by. When this occurs, the tiger beetle larva reaches out and captures it in its sickle-like jaws. It then retreats down into its burrow and eats the captured insect. Then it climbs back up to the tunnel entrance again and waits for another insect to come by.

The forest animals are always hungry and each, in its own way, is always searching for food. Many of the cicada nymphs are captured and eaten by enemies before they can burrow into the ground. Yet, there are so many of them that a few will not be missed.

Even beneath the forest floor there is abundant life of many kinds. Some of these underground animals spend their entire lives there, others remain for only a short time.

Earthworms tunnel along, feeding upon decaying plant material. Only during the nights or when summer showers fall do they come up to the surface.

Plump beetle grubs, too, thrive in the rich soil, feeding upon the roots of plants. In time they will change into winged adult beetles that will leave the ground to mate and lay their eggs.

The caterpillars of some moths feed upon the leaves of the trees, burrowing into the ground when ready to change into inactive pupae. There, fairly safe from enemies and cold, they will remain until another summer arrives. Then they will come up out of the ground as winged moths.

Each creature has its own, special, way of life.

The cicada nymphs that tunnel into the ground have left the sunlit world behind them. Beneath the surface they will dwell in darkness for 17 years. Winters will come and go with their cold and snow, the summers will pass, but most of the nymphs will be safe in their underground realm. Frost can not reach them and they will remain cool even during the hot days of summer.

Each spring, flowers will bloom in the forest and birds will search every leaf and twig for insect food. During all this time the nymphs will live on, unaware of the busy world above them.

Everywhere in the forest the little cicada nymphs are busily digging down through the earth. Using their curved front legs they tunnel down through the soil. Several inches below the surface they stop at last and begin building cells.

In the building of these cells they scrape away bits of soil with their front legs and form them into tiny balls. These are pressed into the walls. While working, they move back and forth but never turn around in their tunnels. Hour after hour they toil until, at last, each nymph has a hollow cell around itself.

The walls of these cells must be made very hard and waterproof. If rainwater should flood them the nymphs would drown.

By the time a day or two have passed most of the nymphs have finished building cells in which they will live for more than a year. Their next, and most important problem is the finding of food.

Each nymph, if it is to survive, must quickly locate a root from which to draw nourishment. Some of the nymphs, more fortunate than others, have built their cells beside roots. Others must dig even farther before finding roots.

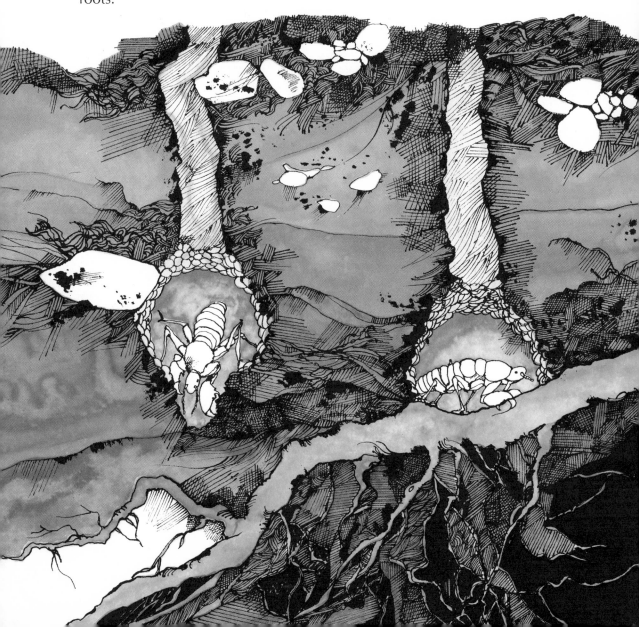

One by one, hidden from the world of sunshine, most of the nymphs are able to locate tree roots. The others die.

In searching for roots the nymphs use their sensitive antennae or feelers. When a living root is found the nymph pushes its sharp beak into it by bracing its body against the wall of its earthen cell.

As soon as the nymph has pierced a root it begins sucking out the nourishing sap flowing through it.

Throughout their nymphal lives beneath the ground, the sap of tree roots will be their only food. Week after week and month after month the little nymphs rest in their cells, slowly pumping out the sap. They grow very slowly. Truly, a young cicada's life seems very dull. Yet, hidden in the ground, they are safe from most enemies.

Time passes and October comes. The sourwoods turn deep red and the maples dress themselves in crimson and gold. Most of the trees along Little River begin dropping their leaves. They fall, one by one, and soon the trees are bare. Gradually the ground becomes carpeted with colorful autumn leaves.

The chipmunks of the valley are even busier than usual. They hurry about through the forest gathering nuts and seeds and carrying them into their burrows. They seem to know that winter is not far off. Many of the birds that have nested in the valley have already flown southward for the winter.

With the arrival of cooler weather the trees stop growing. Now nutritious sap no longer flows through their trunks and roots.

With no root sap to feed upon the cicada nymphs rest quietly in their cells. They will not begin feeding again until spring arrives and sap flows once more through the roots from which they obtain their nourishment.

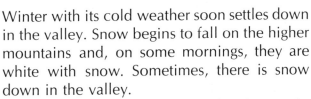

Winter with its cold weather soon settles down in the valley. Snow begins to fall on the higher mountains and, on some mornings, they are white with snow. Sometimes, there is snow down in the valley.

Safe in their underground dens the chipmunks are asleep, often only a few inches away from the cicada nymphs. Unlike some of the other forest creatures they do not remain asleep all winter. They curl up and their breathing slows down. But they wake up now and then and feed upon their stores of food. Then they go to sleep again.

Hanging from the bare limb of an oak tree beside the river there is a large paper nest. During the summer it was the home of several hundred hornets, but it is now deserted. All the worker hornets perished with the arrival of cool weather. Only the young queens remained alive. These left the nest and found places to spend the winter where they would be safe from the cold. When spring comes the queens will revive and each one will build a small paper nest in a tree. By mid-summer these nests will have been made much larger. They will be about a foot in diameter, each one inhabited by a large hornet colony.

Meanwhile beneath the ground, the cicada nymphs rest quietly in their cells. Here they are not concerned with hornets or other enemies. Winter winds may blow and snow may fall but they will be safe from the cold.

Spring comes, at last, to the Great Smoky Mountains. The deep snow on the higher elevations begins to melt and the water flows down the valley in raging torrents. The river overflows its banks and rolls great boulders along in its bed.

Suddenly the valley comes to life, filled with many living things. Tender leaves unfold upon the twigs of the maples, oaks and other trees. Here and there along the river the blooms of dogwoods appear. They are snow-white against the dark forest.

Birds of many kinds have returned from the South and begin building nests in the trees.

Deep in hidden glens along the mountains, mushrooms push up out of the warming earth. They open their parasol-like caps and shed microscopic spores that float away in the breezes. The mushrooms are of almost every hue of the rainbow from deep purple to bright red. In time their spores will come to rest upon the damp earth and germinate. They will grow into masses of underground fungus myclia that will eventually emerge from the ground in the form of mushrooms again.

Warmed by the spring sun, the chipmunks come out of their burrows and once more search for food in the forest.

Sap begins flowing through the trees again, moving slowly through their trunks and through every twig and root.

The cicada nymphs, too, become active and start pumping sap out of the tree roots beside their cells. They begin to grow again.

The cicada nymphs are now slightly larger than they were the previous summer. Their once-slender bodies have expanded so that their skins fit them very tightly.

The time has now arrived for the nymphs to shed their outer skins. Soon the skin of each nymph splits down its back and the insect crawls out of it. Its new skin is slightly larger than its old one and fits it more loosely.

This is the way the little nymphs grow larger. Each time their skins become too tight they are shed. By the time that 17 years have passed they will have shed, or molted, their skins about six times. After each molt they will be a little larger.

And so another summer passes. Nothing much happens to the hidden nymphs. A few are eaten by ants tunneling down through the earth. Once a heavy rain saturates the ground and some of them are drowned. The rest have built harder cells which are waterproof. These nymphs are more fortunate than the rest. As the weeks pass they all continue pumping nutritious sap out of the tree roots through their tube-like beaks.

Another winter comes and they all stop feeding again. For the nymphs, it is the end of another year.

When spring comes again the living things of
the valley revive once more. The nymphs start
feeding and growing. It is the beginning of
their third summer.

Beneath a small, scarlet oak live a large number
of the cicada nymphs, each one quietly sucking sap out of the tree's roots.

Suddenly there is a scratching sound in the
earth but the nymphs do not hear it. They have
no ears.

A mole, blind as are the nymphs, is digging its
tunnel through the ground beneath the oak.
Soon it discovers the hidden nymphs by means
of its long sensitive nose.

The mole pushes slowly through the soft soil
and devours many of the little cicadas. After
awhile it tunnels away, seeking other insects,
such as plump beetle grubs, upon which to
feed.

And so the years slowly pass. Many of the nymphs are eaten by enemies, others are drowned during heavy spring rains.

Every few years, during the summers, the nymphs have molted their skins and grown larger, step by step. Sometimes they have tunneled deeper into the ground and built new, larger, cells. The cells are always located beside tree roots so that they can suck out the sap.

The scene now shifts to an early spring day 17 years after the parent cicadas sang in the sun and laid their eggs in the twigs of the trees along Little River. The nymphs are now more than an inch in length.

Timed, somehow, by their built-in time-clocks, the nymphs are suddenly alerted and begin burrowing upward through the ground.

When the nymphs are about an inch from the surface most of them stop and wait quietly. They are waiting for the time to leave the ground where they have lived and sucked out the sap of tree roots for so many years.

A few of the nymphs, for some unknown reason, build small earthen chimneys extending for several inches above the surface of the ground. These chimneys are hollow but are closed at their tops. Near the base of each one there is a small opening or "window."

Sometimes these chimneys are called "cicada huts."

The mature cicada nymphs hide inside these chimneys or "huts" while waiting for the next chapter in their lives to begin.

May comes once again to Little River Valley and, as usual, the dogwoods open their white blooms. On every tree twig the tightly-rolled buds slowly unfold into thin, blade-like leaves. Birds return and begin building their nests.

The mature cicada nymphs hidden just beneath the surface of the ground or in their "huts" are suddenly alerted, and one warm night they emerge and begin crawling across the forest floor.

The mature nymphs that come up out of the earth are very awkward. They are not accustomed to walking on the ground, so they move very slowly. They wave their crab-like front legs about as they move across the surface of the ground.

A moon hangs above the valley and the only sounds are those of frogs along the river and of a lonely owl calling from far away through the forest.

How the nymphs are aware that the time has come for them to leave the ground, no one knows. But, one by one, they emerge, always doing so at night.

They struggle across the leaf-covered ground until they come to a bush or a tree, then they climb up into it.

When satisfied that they are high enough they anchor their feet on the bark and stop moving. Now they must wait for the next chapter of their lives to begin.

An hour or so passes. The forest is still dark. Down the back of each nymph a seam slowly opens. Soon the insect begins crawling out of its old skin. It must struggle very hard but in time it is free and then rests quietly.

Once out of its nymphal skin the cicada is a far different creature from the one that lived for so long in the earth. At first its body is white and its eyes are bright red. Its wings are soft and limp.

By the time dawn comes to Little River Valley the bodies of the cicadas have become darker and their wings have expanded and hardened. They are now adult cicadas and are nearly ready to fly. Still, they must wait for awhile. Soon the sun rises above the mountains and warms the cicadas perched in the bushes and trees. Suddenly, as if at a given signal, the males all begin sounding their drumming organs. The forest rings, once more, with the sound of singing cicadas.

Again it is a year of the cicadas, a time when they emerge from the earth in great numbers to mate and sing in the summer sun.

During the intervening years, other smaller groups of cicadas have emerged from the earth but never in as large numbers.

This is one of the years when the great cicada throng is timed to appear. Now the males sing in the sun as if trying to make up for their years of silence beneath the ground. The females lay their eggs in the twigs of the trees and another 17 years must pass before the forest along Little River again echoes with cicada song. Thus, does the cicadas' strange life cycle begin again.

SCIENTIFIC NOTES ON CICADAS

Cicadas are large, robust insects, usually more than an inch in length, that spend long periods beneath the ground in their nymphal stages. They vary greatly in coloration; some kinds are tan, others are dark with green, red, or brown markings. They have two pairs of transparent wings and can fly very rapidly. Located upon the males' undersides there are paired drumming organs by means of which they can emit shrill, buzzing sounds that are believed to be mating calls. The females make no sounds.

Cicadas are often called "locusts" but this is incorrect. True locusts belong to the grasshopper family, whereas the cicadas are more closely related to the plant-lice and treehoppers. They have piercing-sucking mouthparts but usually feed very little. The females have spear-like ovipositors or egg-laying tubes which they use to pierce the twigs of trees in order to lay their eggs. When cicadas are abundant the twigs of trees are often severely damaged and many are killed by their egg-laying habits.

After a brief time in the twigs the eggs hatch and the tiny young, or nymphs, drop to the ground and burrow in. In the earth the nymphs construct small cells next to the roots of trees into which they insert their sucking mouthparts. Here, hidden underground, the nymphs live by sucking out the sap of the roots. Now and then they molt their skins as they increase in size. The time spent underground varies with the kind of cicada. Some kinds feed underground for from two to five years. However, the famous 17-year cicadas remain underground for 17 years and occur mostly in the northern portions of the eastern United States. The 13-year cicadas are found in southern areas and spend 13 years in the ground.

The truth is that there are actually six different species, or kinds, all known as *periodical cicadas*. Three kinds spend 17 years underground while the other three kinds spend only 13 years underground. The kind in our story is the common 17-year cicada (*Magicicada septendecim*).

The fact that these unusual insects spend these periods underground does not mean that they appear in forested areas only every 13 or 17 years. They actually emerge somewhere almost every year. This is because there are different groups known as "broods" that overlap in their development. Some of these broods are widely separated geographically; others occur in the same locality, emerging as winged adults after spending their allotted time in the ground. Cicada broods are designated by Roman numerals. The numbering of the broods of 17-year cicadas began in 1893, the first one being known as Brood I. The brood emerging in 1894 was Brood II, and so on through Brood XVII. Brood XVII appeared in 1909 and in 1910 Brood I appeared again.

The numerals XVIII through XXX have been assigned to the various broods of 13-year cicadas. Brood XXX, for example, appeared in 1918, again in 1931, 1944, 1957, and 1970. It will appear again in 1983. As is obvious, the subject is quite complicated and a little difficult to understand.

Brood IX of 17-year cicadas, the one in our story, appeared in 1952, and again in 1969. This same brood will appear again in 1986. However, other smaller broods will probably appear in the localities during the years in between. Other broods of 17-year cicadas will appear in various parts of eastern United States on other years.

Truly, the cicadas are among the most interesting and remarkable of all the world's insects.

INDEX

ABOUT THE AUTHOR AND ARTIST

Ross E. Hutchins can write with authority on the life cycle of the cicada, or any other insect. He was reared on a cattle ranch near Yellowstone National Park and his early interests became centered on the plants and animals of that wild country. For 17 years he was State Entomologist in Mississippi before his resignation in 1968 allowing him to devote his time to writing. The author of 18 books on nature studies and numerous articles in Natural History, National Geographic and other journals, Hutchins holds the Ph.D. from Iowa State University. His hobby, biophotography, is very closely associated with his field of specialization. In fact, many of his books have been illustrated with his own photos. Mr. Hutchins is a member of the American Entomological Society, Sigma XI, Phi Kappa Phi, and the Authors Guild.

Arvis L. Stewart's special interests include printmaking, carpentry, and natural history, as evidenced by his drawing. He is a graduate of Texas Technological College. Mr. Stewart has illustrated several other Addisonian Press Books, two of which are MY GOLDFISH and ANIMAL HABITATS: WHERE CAN RED-WINGED BLACKBIRDS LIVE?